FIRST
IN WEST YORKSHIRE

THE HISTORY OF EZRA LAYCOCK OF COWLING

PHILIP LINGARD

TURNTABLE PUBLICATIONS
SHEFFIELD

85p

OTHER TRANSPORT TITLES

Buses in Leeds
Memories of Grimsby and Cleethorpes Transport
Edinburgh Tramways Album
Scottish Buses Before 1928
Leeds City Tramways
Historic Commercial Vehicles
Scottish Electric Tramways

© 1975 Philip Lingard

ISBN 0 902844 28 8

Printed by Crown Press (Keighley) Ltd., Chapel Lane, Keighley
West Yorkshire

FOREWORD

It has been my aim in compiling this brief history to present a true and accurate picture of the operations and some of the personalities involved in the small concern of Ezra Laycock. Unlike rail closures, which leave a legacy of old track bed, cuttings, embankments and other permanent or semi-permanent features, once a bus service ceases, there are only the memories of past passengers and drivers, the occasional press-cutting and the odd official document to serve as reminders of its former existence. During my research, these leads were frequently contradictory so that in many instances, the book recounts the most likely sequence of events, considering the amazing frequency of route commencements, alterations and abandonments during the 1920s. Indeed, the claim that Laycock's ran the first motor bus in Yorkshire has been challenged by evidence of a similar machine crashing on Knaresborough Hill in 1902! However, such evidence is largely circumstantial and there is no shadow of a doubt that a Milnes-Daimler single-decker made a triumphal arrival at Cowling early in 1905, and was hailed first of its ilk.

My thanks for helping with the research go to Mr C. A. L. Wright, who also provided several introductions and many of the photos from his collection, to Mr K. Brigg for his fascinating recollections of working for Laycock's in the 1920s, and to Mr R. Stapleton for sharing his experiences as a Laycock driver in the 1930s and 1940s. BBC Radio Blackburn, the Burnley Evening Star and Dalesman Magazine kindly published my appeals for information to which many people, too numerous to mention individually, replied, and I am most grateful. The Keighley News and Yorkshire Evening Post provided material for publication and Mr D. W. Chaplin, General Manager of the Burnley, Colne and Nelson Joint Transport Committee and Mr R. Marshall, General Manager of Burnley and Pendle, generously provided many of the few extant official records of Laycock's. Finally, my thanks to Messrs R. Jackson and C. Nuttall for supplying the remainder of the photographs, to Mr J. Cockshott for reviewing the fleet list, to my parents for their encouragement and to the Laycock family and Mr R. Laycock in particular, for their help.

January 1975.   P. Lingard

A general view of Cowling Garage taken in 1921. Seen from left to right, the vehicles are: the Commer 3P, the Leyland charabanc with hood raised, the original Milnes-Daimler at the ripe old age of 16 and the Commer double-decker. It is not known whether the cars in the background were owned by Laycocks. (Keighley News)

THE HISTORY OF EZRA LAYCOCK

The coming of the railways ended much of the isolation of the Yorkshire Dales during the mid-19th Century, but it was not until the first horse buses arrived, fifty years later, that numerous outlying villages became readily accessible. One such community was Cowling, in South Craven, which is situated on the road between Cross Hills and Colne. One hundred years ago, this now busy thoroughfare was little more than an ill-drained cart track, frequented only by the occasional horse and wary pedestrians.

During the 1880s the village postman was a Mr Ezra Laycock. Every day he walked to the mail delivery limit in Cross Hills and returned the three miles up the valley, carrying all the letters and parcels for delivery in Cowling. Like most Yorkshiremen of his day, Ezra Laycock was a very shrewd, broad-spoken man, who rarely missed an opportunity to better himself. In 1890, after much persuasion, he purchased his father-in-law's business as village coal merchant. The regular visits to Kildwick Railway Station had always made carriage of general merchandise for the villagers a profitable side-line, so on the acquisition of the horse and cart, Ezra combined his three jobs in one; Kildwick and Cross Hills being adjoining villages.

For some years, a number of Cowling's inhabitants, compelled to find employment outside the village, had either to walk, or share the horse and trap, which one of them owned, to reach the station. Ezra had always given lifts to any villager he had encountered struggling to or from Kildwick and so it was mooted that the horse and trap, which stood idle at the station all day, awaiting the return of its occupants, be placed at his disposal. Ezra readily accepted the offer and the business expanded, diversifying into marriage and funeral transport at the same time. In 1895, sufficient passenger traffic was carried to warrant the purchase of a waggonette, whilst in recognition of the volume of business generated in Cowling, the Midland Railway Company appointed Ezra Laycock as their parcel agent in the village. Over the ensuing decade, the business continued to grow until, at one time, the stables housed twelve horses and several gigs and waggonettes, one of which seated over 20 passengers. In the morning and evening, even this capacity was insufficient and boys going to or from Glusburn School had to ride on the tail-board, or be "whipped behind" as it was known.

However, Ezra had been so successful that he attracted competitors, who, debarred from carrying parcels for the railway under the agency scheme, started vying for passengers between Cowling and Kildwick. True to character, Ezra was prepared to use any means to combat the newcomers, but despite buying faster and faster horses to speed his passengers to their destinations, his custom waned and he was forced to sell most of his waggonettes.

Whilst running a group of businessmen to Kildwick Station to catch the Bradford train, Ezra first heard of the motor buses that a

London operator was experimenting with. Believing this to be the answer to his rivals, he went into partnership with a mechanically-minded man from Skipton — a Mr Stephenson. Early in 1905, Ezra and his eldest son, Rennie, who was only 15, embarked on a remarkable expedition by Edwardian standards, travelling to London in search of a motor bus. The two walked the streets of London for three days, seeing nothing more modern than hosts of double-deck horse-drawn buses. Following a tip that there were some motorised vehicles in Brighton, they bought a half-day excursion ticket to that Sussex resort. As they returned to the railway station, exhausted and disappointed after a fruitless search, they caught a glimpse of a motor bus passing the end of the street. The two Yorkshiremen could only stay a few moments longer, but what they had seen had convinced Ezra that the solution to his problems was at hand.

Thus, Laycock and Stephenson of Cowling contacted Messrs Milnes-Daimler and Co., to place an order for one single-deck vehicle. The origins of the supplier were difficult to trace because many manufacturers embodied Daimler in their title, it being as synonymous with the internal combustion engine as Hoover is with vacuum-cleaners today. This particular company was formed as a result of an agreement in November 1902 between G. F. Milnes and Co., of Hadley, Shropshire, a famous manufacturer of trams, horse-buses and railway rolling stock and the Daimler Motoren-Gesellschaft, in Germany, to construct motor vehicles for the United Kingdom. It was in no way related to the famous Daimler Co. in Coventry, which is now a subsidiary of British Leyland.

A privileged party of eighteen, including Mr & Mrs Laycock and Mr & Mrs W. Stephenson, travelled to London where the body was being built for the vehicle. Three days after their arrival the bus was completed and the eighteen hardy travellers embarked on what was to become the longest journey made by motorbus in England up to that date. The story is told by Mr Frank Driver who, on the golden anniversary of the occasion, was interviewed by the Yorkshire Evening Post, whose management has generously permitted me to reproduce the conversation:-

"I was a weaving overlooker in Cowling at the time and a comedian and a nigger minstrel at local concerts. Ezra asked me along so I could do a bit of entertaining for the party during the nights we were in lodgings.

"We stayed at Lavender Hill, London, and each morning went along to watch the bus being finished. When it was ready we had a test of hill-climbing at Brighton, because Ezra knew that what was good enough for flat country might not be any good for our hills at home.

"We watched the bus go up the hill alright and Ezra said to me, 'That'll do for me Frank. We'll have t'bus'.

"It was the first time I'd been to Brighton so I asked him if we were going to stay a bit and have a look around. Ezra said, 'We're not, lad. Business is business. Let's get back to Cowling'.

"We started on the Thursday afternoon at five o'clock and stayed the night at Hitchin, 35 miles away in Hertfordshire. Next day we went up the Great North Road and at every place we passed through, the folks were lining the streets, shouting and waving. They had never seen a motor bus before.

"We only had one spot of trouble. That was at Doncaster, where the bush on one wheel got a bit hot and a policeman came and said it was making a bit of a stink. But he'd never seen a motorbus before, either, so he didn't know what to do about it.

"We stayed the night at Doncaster and we went on to Bradford, where we registered the bus. Then it was off home to Cowling. They gave us a grand welcome that Saturday afternoon. The whole village turned out."

The arrival at Kildwick coincided with the departure of a horse-drawn service, so in order to afford his regular clientele their first motorised ride to Cowling, the two vehicles exchanged loads. The horses raced ahead, warning the village of the impending homecoming of Ezra's bus. As it turned into the stables, the entire population of 1,000 were there, shouting, cheering and waving, welcoming their new bus in a manner befitting Royalty.

By modern standards the "Monster", as it became known, was extremely primitive, containing numerous technical defects, but fortunately, most of these could be rectified fairly quickly when the vehicle broke down. The body was constructed entirely of wood and afforded no protection from the elements to the driver and little to the passengers, but as the horse buses offered similar standards, there

AK335 photographed en route from London to Cowling.
(Bob Jackson)

Laycock & Stephenson,

MOTOR BUS

AND

CAR PROPRIETORS,

COWLING.

Will run Busses at the following times from

Oct. 1st, 1905, to March 31st, 1906.

NOTICE

Busses will stop at the following places to pick up and set down passengers: Flood Root, Gibb Street, Sun Street, Green Street, Bay Horse Inn, Crag View, Garden Terrace, Lane Ends. Glusburn: Green Lane, Temperance Hotel, Institute. Crosshills: Towning Place, Sutton Lane End, Craven Bank, and Kildwick Station.

We should esteem it a favour if passengers would kindly observe these stopping places.

Every endeavour will be made to run Busses as shewn in Time Table, but we do not hold ourselves responsible for loss or inconvenience caused by Busses not running in accordance with this Time Table.

Thanking you for past patronage, and trusting you for the future,

We remain,

Yours sincerely,

LAYCOCK & STEPHENSON.

TIME TABLE.

Day	Leave Cowling for Kildwick	Leave Kildwick for Cowling	Leave Cowling for Laneshawbridge	Leave Laneshawbridge for Cowling
SUNDAY	8-50 a.m. 1-40 p.m. 5-0 ,, 7-15 ,,	9-20 a.m. 2-5 p.m. 5-25 ,, 7-50 ,,	9-40 a.m. 2-30 p.m. 5-45 ,, 8-15 ,,	10-10 a.m. 3-10 p.m. 6-10 ,, 8-40 ,,
MONDAY	7-45 a.m. 9-30 ,, 1-0 p.m. 3-45 ,, 5-50 ,,	8-10 a.m. 10-5 ,, 2-11 p.m. 4-45 ,, 6-35 ,,		
TUESDAY	7-45 a.m. 9-30 ,, 1-0 p.m. 3-45 ,, 5-50 ,, 9-0 ,,	8-10 a.m. 10-5 ,, 2-11 p.m. 4-45 ,, 6-35 ,, 9-58 ,,		
WEDNES.	7-45 a.m. 9-30 ,, 1-0 p.m. 3-45 ,, 5-50 ,, 8-0 ,,	8-10 a.m. 10-5 ,, 2-11 p.m. 4-45 ,, 6-35 ,, 8-30 ,,		
THURSDAY	7-45 a.m. 9-30 ,, 1-0 ,, 3-45 p.m. 5-50 ,, 8-0 ,,	8-10 a.m. 10-5 ,, 2-11 p.m. 4-45 ,, 6-35 ,, 8-30 ,,		
FRIDAY	7-45 a.m. 9-30 ,, 1-0 p.m. 3-45 ,, 5-50 ,,	8-10 a.m. 10-5 ,, 1-5 p.m. 2-11 ,, 4-45 ,, 6-35 ,,		
SATURDAY	7-45 a.m. 9-30 ,, 11-55 ,, 1-0 p.m. 2-0 ,, 3-45 ,, 5-30 ,, 8-0 ,, 9-0 ,, 10-50 ,,	8-10 a.m. 10-5 ,, 12-35 p.m 2-11 ,, 2-50 ,, 4-45 ,, 6-35 ,, 8-30 ,, 9-58 ,, 11-20 ,,	1-0 p.m. 7-5 ,,	1-30 p.m. 7-30 ,,

were no complaints. The vehicle stood 2ft 10ins from the ground with solid tyres on wheels of 32ins diameter at the front and 42ins diameter at the rear. Overall length was 19ft 11ins and the width only 6ft 6ins. The engine is quoted as being of 30 hp — usually fitted to double-deckers, with a 20 hp unit being standard in the single-deck. Obviously, Ezra had taken the Pennines into consideration! There were no sparking plugs in the engine, as a method employing low tension ignition, utilising a spark in the cylinders to explode the petrol vapour, was used. The petrol was carried at the rear of the chassis, some exhaust gas being diverted to the tank to create enough pressure to raise the fuel to the carburettor. There were three levers for changing gear and final drive was achieved by means of a cast iron circular rack, bolted to the rear wheels. All in all, the "Monster" was something of a mechanical wonder for 1905.

Certainly the locals had little but praise for the bus for, despite dire prophecies of lack of support and ceaseless mechanical failure, from equestrian-minded rivals, Ezra's bus was in such heavy demand by private hire parties that it was over a month before it made its first advertised stage service run. It was even loaned to the Local Authority at Yeadon for a week, for use on the very hilly access roads to the village. The seven days were too short for the curious villagers, the bus coming through with shining colours! One journey on the Feast Sunday of July 1905 was to Nelson, where the police had to clear a route through the dense crowds which had gathered. Wherever it travelled, crowds hurried to catch a glimpse of it, chil-

The many antiquated features of the first Milnes-Daimler are well seen in this view, including the acetylene lamps, the bulb horn, a very ornate luggage rack and the brake-shoes applied directly on to the solid rear wheels. (Keighley News)

dren and even dogs being held aloft to gain a better view, such was the attraction of Ezra's bus.

By September, the novelty had worn thin and the Milnes-Daimler reverted to toiling its way between Kildwick and Cowling as intended, with occasional journeys over the county border to Laneshaw Bridge, the tramway terminus for Colne. The uniqueness also vanished quickly as, in the Autumn of 1905, the Silsden Motor Bus Company Ltd. took delivery of a motor vehicle, heralded by the Silsden Brass Band, which played it up the road to the village. In 1906, they were joined by Mr C. Chapman of Grassington, who began the replacement of his horse-drawn mail buses between Skipton and Upper Wharfedale by motor vehicles. However, neither Chapman's nor the Silsden Motor Bus Co. survived into the thirties as the former was taken over by the rapidly expanding West Yorkshire Road Car Co. Ltd., and the latter went bankrupt.

Thus, the gamble by Laycock and Stephenson had succeeded. The "Monster" was not without flaw, clutch-slip being the most common ailment and frequently the passengers were delayed thirty minutes as the driver knelt under his vehicle putting fuller's earth, or sand, into the offending clutch. However, even this was insufficient to deter willing customers and the business entered a new era of prosperity and security.

Ezra Laycock is photographed here at the wheel of the original single-decker with a party of villagers from Cowling. The second body was ideal for outings with its open sides and stepped seating. In comparison with the earlier view, many mechanical alterations had been made, notably the repositioning of the brakes. (Keighley News)

The Summer of 1905 must have been unusually hot, as a second body was built for the Milnes-Daimler, the first being deemed too enclosed, but as it was entirely open, both front and rear, it is hard to see why. The second body, constructed by Laycock and Stephenson, broke new ground by including 25 forward facing seats, gently inclined from front to rear, as opposed to the 18 inward facing seats fitted previously. The passengers enjoyed clear views on all sides, only the rear being enclosed. However, during inclement weather, protection was afforded by the canvas roof and drop-roll side curtains. A similar design was being used by Leyland for their first motor buses. Later developments in 1907 were the provision of a windscreen and the abandonment of braking on the surface of the tyres — as in horse vehicle practice — in favour of brake shoes acting against the inner rims of the rear wheels. From photographic evidence it appears that the first body was retained for Winter use, to be replaced by the second in Summer. This was common practice in those days, when haulage firms built charabanc bodies to fit to their lorries in Summer. Numerous bus companies, both large and small, originated in this manner.

On 17th February 1906, a second Milnes-Daimler was delivered, which dwarfed even the first "Monster". Seating 49, three passengers were carried on a bench next to the driver, five sat in a smoking compartment immediately behind (a similar arrangement was the open rear platform on the first body of the single decker), 16 in the remainder of the lower saloon and 25 on the wholly-exposed upper deck. A local wag claimed that more people alighted from the vehicle on one occasion than could fit into the first Keighley cinema. As

The first double-decker was delivered early in 1906 and was one of the earliest to be motor propelled.   (Bob Jackson)

Traffic Regulations were few in those days, the bus worked to overcapacity and apparently did so in safety. Again Ezra was pioneering, as this was claimed to be amongst the first half-dozen motorised double-deckers ever built.

This second vehicle was more difficult to obtain, as the three largest London companies were buying every motorbus produced for the British market. At the end of 1905 there were only twenty such vehicles in London, but in 1908, when the London General Omnibus Co. merged with its two largest rivals, there were 1,066. Ezra was now able to employ a driver and conductor to man his first two vehicles, which worked between Kildwick and Cowling for over 14 years.

Although motor coach tours did not begin on any scale until after the First World War, Laycock and Stephenson did much pioneering work. Each St Ledger Day, the fully laden double-deck bus made a pilgrimage to Doncaster, quite a momentous journey in those days. In vindicating its preference for horse-drawn waggonettes, an issue of the "Ilkley Gazette" in May 1907, referred to a Sunday outing to Knaresborough and Harrogate by 30 Barnoldswick men in a Laycock and Stephenson motor bus, which broke down at midnight on reaching Ilkley. The driver took two hours, vainly trying to remedy the defect, but it was not until the local mechanic had been roused and his ingenuity brought to bear that the vehicle returned to life. This accomplished, the irate but tired passengers could do little but murmur at the prospect of staying the rest of the night in Ilkley.

Two ex-London taxis were acquired by the business to replace the remaining gigs, followed, probably in early 1908, by a magnificent motor brougham. Resplendent in its all-white livery, in contrast to the normal dark green, it was a 25 or 30 hp Maudslay 30-seater. Its first assignment was to convey the wedding party of Ezra's eldest daughter — conforming to his belief that every development of the business should coincide with a unique family occasion. The new vehicle also relieved Ezra of his self-imposed task of bringing the doctor from Cross Hills to Cowling. Regardless of weather and time, he could be relied upon, sometimes having to give assistance with maternity cases. On one occasion, when the only horse in the stables was lame, he ran the distance to summon aid.

The pre-war fleet was completed sometime in 1910, when a second 50-seat open-top double-decker was bought from the London General Omnibus Company. Little is known about this bus, but it was pressed into service on the Cowling-Kildwick route with the earlier double-decker. This was the solution to all load fluctuations and, although they would be hard-pressed to overtake the horse-drawn waggonettes which they replaced, their passenger potential seemed inexorable. The double-deckers became known to their schoolboy passengers as "Tinker" and "Slasher" and their crews were local heroes. The fares the conductor collected were 3d to Cross Hills (down) and 4d from Cross Hills (up). Hence the distance to Cowling has always been known as "four miles there and three miles back"!

The first Laycock and Stephenson charabanc was this 1908 Maudslay. It was photographed (resplendent in its all white livery) at Kildwick Cross Roads. (Bob Jackson)

After 1912 many changes came over the business. Mr Stephenson left and his place taken by Ezra's two sons, John and Rennie. However, on the outbreak of the First World War they joined the Army Transport Corps, the experience from which undoubtedly enabled them to survive the fierce competition of the twenties. Prior to 1914, the morning bus for workers from Cowling set off to repeated honkings of the huge bulb horn until every one of the regular passengers was aboard, but with the disappearance of much of the local workforce to the trenches, that particular aspect of the service ceased, never to be resumed. Coach tours also came to an untimely halt and the charabanc and the ex-LGOC double-decker were requisitioned by the War Department.

However, the years of stagnation during the War did not affect Ezra's lust for pioneering. Anticipating a quick resurgence of motor excursions, he purchased a magnificent Maudslay luxury coach. The 32 seats were fully upholstered, whilst in bad weather the canvas roof was unrolled and the passengers stayed warm and dry in the enclosed saloon. Again, the inauguration proved memorable. Fully-laden, the coach departed to Carsethorne, near Dumfries in Scotland, to visit Ezra's brother. It returned in triumph, the occupants full of stories of their adventures and weighed down by fresh salmon taken from the waters of the Solway Firth. Custom on the stage service also quickly revived and two Commers, one a chain-driven double-decker and the other a 32-seat single-decker, with bevel-drive, were bought. Contrary to photographic evidence, tax records suggest that the former was delivered as a 30-seat single-decker and altered to double-deck in April 1923. It could be that these records are incorrect, or that two bodies were used and the double-deck version only recorded in 1923. These new vehicles replaced the original Milnes-Daimlers which had each run 300,000 miles by 1920. Despite becoming uneconomical, because of newly-introduced petrol taxes, this make of vehicle was probably the most reliable and efficient of the Edwardian era and served all its operators well.

The private hire side of the business expanded rapidly and new Leyland and Ford charabancs were assisted by secondhand Lancia, Talbot, Daimler and Bean vehicles, whilst a Belsize maintained the Laycock presence in taxis. However, competition once again became fierce as many officers returning from the War bought small, fast American buses to win passengers from established operators. Huge numbers of surplus army lorries were being sold and many were rebodied and pressed into service as buses. The now-nationalised Ribble Motor Services started operations with 12 such reconditioned vehicles in the Preston area in 1919. Reflecting these trends, Laycock and Sons bought a small-capacity bus in 1924, for use on a new Cowling-Skipton service, which was withdrawn three years later. This vehicle, a Reo, manufactured in the USA, was particularly popular with the British "pirate" operators, being sold under such names as Speedwagon, Sprinter, Major, Pullman and Gold Crown, titles which their performance ably matched.

By 1925, Ezra decided that the fleet had become sufficiently large to warrant the use of fleet numbers. It is thought that he counted the number of motor vehicles previously owned and thus numbered his next vehicle, a Morris taxi, No. 16. However, the author's research indicates that he had already operated 18 buses, charabancs and taxis. Several years later, when queried on this point, John Laycock drew up his list of Laycock's fleet to that date, omitting the ex-LGOC double-decker and the two Maudslay's. Why, remains a mystery.

A Standard taxi, numbered 17 in 1925, brought the number of purchases since the War to 14. It is interesting to note in these days of standardisation that they were supplied by 13 different manufacturers and even the two Commers differed significantly!

Until 1926, one of the most worrying aspects of the business for Ezra was the fact that licensing agreements prevented his vehicles from operating into Colne and Keighley. Beyond Laneshaw Bridge, Colne Corporation trams connected with his services and Keighley Corporation trolleybuses provided the other link at Cross Hills. However, during the General Strike, in May 1926, the workers of those two bodies supported their Union's call for action. It is not known whether Ezra took the initiative to extend his route into the two towns, but police protection was given and a promise made that he could continue the service on a permanent basis on return to normal conditions. Thus, his buses ran the gauntlet for the duration of the strike and were a prime target for the abuse and stones thrown by the strikers.

Commer double-decker WRI622 is shown here at Kildwick Railway Station collecting passengers for the journey to Cowling.
(Keighley News)

The Leyland charabanc is seen on a packed outing in the early 1920s. In bad weather the hood could be raised as depicted on the frontispiece. (Keighley News)

An ornate carved roof and intricate "lining-out" were the most interesting features of this Commer 3P, pictured outside the Laycock garage in Cowling. (Keighley News)

Smaller than the Leyland was this Talbot Charabanc, manufactured by a firm more famous for the many successful racing cars it produced. However, the maximum speed of this vehicle was only 12 mph.
(Keighley News)

However, at the termination of the strike, the agreement between the parties was so altered by the municipalities that if Laycock's took advantage of the route extensions, every other operator's application for a licence between Colne and Keighley would be granted. Ezra knew that circumstances were such that his business would not be able to survive the competition which would ensue, and made an embittered plea for a return to the original agreement. Local MPs took up his case and the dispute became the subject of a lengthy debate in Parliamentary circles with questions raised in the House of Commons, but all to no avail.

Competition for routes at this time became keener than ever. Local authorities began operating motor and trolleybuses to support their waning tram networks and large company monopolies were growing, swallowing innumerable tiny operators, which were often unsound, both financially and mechanically. In order to bring some sanity into the situation, the Ministry of Transport was created which, whilst doing much to control the dangerous competition for the benefit of companies and passengers alike, could not help but complicate matters with "red tape". Laycocks quickly realised that their only chance of success was expansion into more rural areas where the powerful national and municipal operators had less interest.

In October 1925, Laycocks had taken delivery of a Maudslay single-deck bus number 18 and subsequently placed an order for two more for use on the proposed route extension, during the General Strike. Because of their quicker deliveries Maudslay of Alcester, Worcestershire, were chosen by Ezra in preference to Leyland who built vehicles with similar mechanical refinements. Thus in June 1926, numbers 19 and 20 were delivered, with bodies removed from vehicles owned by Wright Bros. of Burnley. All three were of the ML4/26 variety with a wheel base of 15ft 2ins and were propelled by a 4.06 litre Maudslay petrol engine, mounted together with the gear box at a backward tilt to enable direct transmission to the rear axle. These buses were noted for their speed, so it was fortunate that four wheel brakes were provided. The 26-seat bodies each had a character of its own, number 18 in particular was unusual in that it tapered both fore and aft, gaining the nickname of the "Coffin"; whilst number 19 stood so high off the ground that three black rocker panels similar to those on the trams were fitted to prevent children and animals from crawling underneath. In January 1927, two more Maudslays were delivered, followed by a sixth in October of the same year.

On the 25th July 1927, Ezra embarked on a policy of expansion, accepting an offer from Colne Corporation of the Colne-Keighley route. Colne Corporation, operating Guys and Leylands and the West Yorkshire Road Car Company, operating Tilling-Stevens, had already commenced operation on the 1st of April and the three ran the route on a joint rather than a competitive basis. As a result, the Laneshaw Bridge-Kildwick service was withdrawn.

During 1926 and 1927, Laycocks bombarded Colne Corporation with route applications, all of which were refused, with the exception of one from Colne to Cowling via Earby, Skipton and Kildwick. This application was made on 9th May 1927, with the permission of Earby U.D.C., and not having received a reply, Ezra Laycock and Sons commenced the service on 25th July, the same date as they began the Colne-Keighley route. The following day the request was refused, but the service continued whilst an appeal — which proved successful — was made to the Ministry of Transport. This route ran in direct competition with Corporation buses which had started operation between Colne and Earby on the 27th January 1923. Early in 1927, Ribble Motor Services Ltd reached Skipton, with the acquisition of Castle Motors and followed this, on 1st September in the same year, with a Skipton-Colne route, despite opposition from Earby U.D.C. Laycocks subsequently suffered combined opposition through an agreement between Ribble Motor Services and Colne Corporation to eliminate competition. They were unfortunate in that whereas most large operators did not absorb many independents until the early 1930s, Ribble pursued a very aggressive take-over policy from an early date. The problems of such operators as Laycocks were further compounded in 1928, when railways were permitted to take financial interests in bus companies, the largest of which now availed themselves of the capital with which to expand.

Because of the length of time that has passed since the ensuing disputes between Laycocks and Colne Corporation, many official records have been destroyed and the accounts and independent reports which do remain differ substantially on several points. However, it is clear that despite abandoning the Skipton-Cowling section late in 1927, Laycocks' buses were still severely impeded by Colne Corporation. Vehicles were prohibited from picking up passengers in Colne who hadn't previously booked and the terminus had to be altered three times. Between the 7th and 25th of January 1928, the route had to terminate at the borough boundary and when an acceptable stop was located in Colne, Police Sergeant Smith, of the Colne Constabulary, threatened to prosecute Laycocks under a bye-law which, after consultation with Mr Nutter, the then Town Clerk, apparently did not exist! Difficulties were also encountered with Ribble, between Thornton and Skipton, but after a brief withdrawal the service was reinstated on 13th February 1928. Despite its troubled history, during their first 16 months operation of the route, Laycocks' buses carried 401,488 fare-paying passengers, excluding the weekly pass holders, which usually numbered around 100.

To cope with these additional passengers, two Maudslay ML3/35s were delivered early in 1928. These two 32-seaters were notable in that they were the first forward control vehicles bought by Laycocks, i.e. the driver was seated over the front axle, to the left of the engine. Further 1928 acquisitions were three Dennis Gs, two of which had been supplied new to Premier, of Earby, and the third ordered by them. The take-over of Premier, on the 25th March 1928, brought the Barnoldswick-Skipton routes under Laycocks' control. However, it was a move with a large element of risk attached, as anybody could have started operation on the run without attracting the attention of

Photographed in Cowling are these five Maudslays. From left to right they are ML4s 29, 18 (the "coffin"), ML3s 34, 20 and another ML4.

Photographed from left to right are: Dennis Gs 27, 28, Maudslay ML4 number 20, Commer 35, Maudslay 23 and another ML4.

the licensing authorities. Two routes were operated, each at an hourly frequency, one via West Marton and the other, more direct, through Thornton. In addition, a return trip up Tubber Hill was made during the gap between services, at the Barnoldswick end of the route, whilst when returning to, or coming from the garage, buses traversed the unmade road to Earby.

At the completion of a successful 1928, marred only by the continued opposition of Colne Corporation, Laycock and Sons ran 15 vehicles — two 32-seat Maudslays, six 26-seat Maudslays, one 26-seat Maudslay all-weather coach, three 20-seat Dennis's, one 20-seat Albion, one 6-seat Austin and a 4-seat Morris car, the total Road Fund Tax paid being £779.

During 1929, two more Maudslays were delivered. No. 31, an ML3/35, was delivered in March and was unusual in that its 32-seat Barton and Danson body had two doors, one at the front and one situated at the back behind the rear axle. This experiment was not repeated, despite the advantage of shorter stops, as too many passengers were able to evade fare payment. The second, No. 32, was to all accounts a beautiful machine. It carried 26-seat, all-weather coachwork by London Lorries fitted to an ML6/30 chassis. The 6-cylinder engine had a capacity of 7.4 litres, enabling it to be the fastest coach in the fleet. Until its withdrawal in 1934, it was known to all the drivers as the "flyer" and was said to be able to catch pigeons on the wing.

Late in 1929 the road between Salterforth and Barnoldswick was metalled and a new bridge built across the canal. Taking advantage of this facility, Ezra Laycock and Sons instituted an Earby-Klondyke-Salterforth-Barnoldswick-Coates service on Christmas Eve 1929. A Barnoldswick-Salterforth-Colne service was also introduced, but this was withdrawn in favour of an extension of the Earby route to Colne soon after, because of competition from the Ribble route between Colne and Barnoldswick via Standing Stone Gate and the poor road surface between Salterforth and Kelbrook.

During 1930, two Commers joined the Laycock fleet. Their 20-seat Barnaby bodies were fitted to lorry chassis, which lacked spring suspension at the rear, thus giving an unusually hard ride, even for 1930. On one occasion, John Laycock was driving an evening bus from Skipton when he noticed a gentleman in a bowler hat bouncing up and down on the rear seat as the Commer negotiated the poor road surface of Marton Lane. As the Southfield hump-back bridge over the canal was approached, he accelerated. The man was thrown out of his seat and hit his head on the roof, forcing his hat down over his eyes. On arrival at Barnoldswick, John was still laughing to himself as his passenger struggled to remove the firmly-lodged hat! The Commer displaced the two ex-Premier Dennis Gs which, by March 1932, were operating with A. F. England of Luton, appropriately, trading as Union Jack. In 1933 Union Jack's routes were taken over by Luton Corporation, with whom the Dennis Gs operated until 1938, when they returned to Union Jack, which was by then operating as a dealer.

During the early days of the routes to Earby, competition was not confined to Ribble and Colne Corporation. Ezra realised that the local population had to learn to use the motor bus, as opposed to the trains operated by the L.M.S. between Skipton and Colne and on the Earby-Barnoldswick branch line. Amongst his most ingenious publicity ideas was to equip all his distinctive dark green buses with green lights on the roof. A sustained advertising campaign was launched in his time and fare tables, encouraging people to "Travel on the bus with the green light". However, the L.M.S. objected, on the grounds that locomotive drivers in Earby Station could mistake the green lights on the buses, in the adjacent road, for green signals at night. In order to avoid allegations of disregard for safety, the offending lights were removed. Subsequently, a Maudslay was fitted with a blind which not only included the destination but the title "E. Laycock and Sons". This too was unsuccessful, as the overall effect was deemed too cramped.

By 1930, the British Electric Traction Co., which controlled Ribble and Thomas Tilling, and British Automobile Traction Co., which controlled West Yorkshire, had divided the country into areas, where it was agreed that one company could run a subsidiary without competition from the other. One boundary passed through Skipton and the Ribble service to Embsay violated the agreement, so it was to be expected that when Ribble extended to Bolton Abbey, West Yorkshire would operate a service in competition. The resulting friction rendered Winter operations so uneconomical that both routes were withdrawn and Laycocks stepped into the breach by providing a service.

Prior to 1930, the regulations governing the operation of the bus industry were contained in an array of 19th century legislation for the control of horse-drawn vehicles, the most important being the 1832 Stage Carriage Act and the Town Police Clauses Acts of 1847 and 1889. They contained many anomalies such as being applicable only to vehicles plying for hire on the streets, thus exempting all services which used private land as termini. More important so far as Laycocks were concerned, the Town Police Clauses Acts were both permissive and flexible, and being administered by Local Authorities, resulted in licences being sought in each town of operation. Municipalities with their own transport undertakings, such as Colne, were particularly hostile to independents, whilst frequently in county districts, authorities did not issue licences, thus placing existing operators in constant peril from competition on their rural routes. However, the Road Traffic Act passed in 1930 created a new ordered framework by establishing thirteen Traffic Areas which were later abridged to twelve. The Traffic Commissioners were responsible through their Vehicle Examiners for issuing Certificates of Fitness for Passenger Service Vehicles and were empowered, through hearings at their courts, which were organised on lines broadly similar to Courts of Justice, with a system of appeals to the Minister of Transport, to licence routes for stage and express carriage services, excursions and tours, and to approve timetables and fares.

The first sitting of the Traffic Commissioners was in Nottingham in April 1931, the intention being to issue licences automatically to the established operators of a route, providing that their vehicles carried Certificates of Fitness, and an all-year-round service was running to a fixed timetable. Where such monopoly powers granted were abused, individual vehicle or carriage licences, or in extreme circumstances, all the licences held by an individual operator, could be revoked. Thus, Ezra Laycock and Sons were granted licences for all their services, including the Bolton Abbey route. It is interesting to note that in the majority of rural areas where former Tilling and B.E.T. firms met, numerous independent operators still exist, often because the large operators were not prepared to provide a Winter service in 1930.

Laycocks' last Maudslays were delivered early in 1932, replacing the Commers and the last Dennis and bringing the fleet strength to 16 buses and a car, a total never to be attained again. The new vehicles were ML3/35s, fitted with 32-seat bodies built by Barnaby, of Hull. Despite being numbered 36-38 they were always referred to as 17, 18 and 19, because of their unusual registrations: YG 17-19. The first Maudslays continued to give good service, though their original bodies had worn out. 19 was again fitted with a body taken from a Wright Bros. Leyland, whilst 18, 20 and 22 were fitted with Knape bodies, removed from McCurds owned by Claremont, prior to their take-over by Ribble. The original body fitted to 23 had not decayed as fast as the others and was kept until withdrawal, unlike that on 21, which suffered the sorry fate of being destroyed in a fire at Broughton. However, the chassis was recovered and a magnificent Bellhouse-Hartwell body, which embodied luxurious seating and a green roof light — a very advanced feature in those days — was built for it.

From 1929 the Great Depression affected Colne and the Craven area. Unemployment soared, particularly in the cotton towns, with a devastating effect on the Laycock business. They were no longer able to compete successfully for passengers between Colne and Earby and this section was withdrawn early in 1932, buses now terminating at the Red Lion Hotel, in Earby. The Tubber Hill and Coates routes in Barnoldswick also ceased operation. However, these economies could not save the business, which was rapidly going bankrupt, through substantial losses on every route. As a result, it was reluctantly decided to sell out and Ribble Motor Services was approached, but even this small company was badly affected by the slump and did not wish to acquire more services operating at a deficit.

The Colne Corporation Act of 1933 constituted the Burnley, Colne and Nelson Joint Transport Committee by merging the separate municipal undertakings of the three towns. Protracted negotiations were opened with this body, resulting in the eventual sale of the Laycock business. There is evidence that B.C.N. buses started replacing Laycocks' vehicles on the Colne-Keighley and Skipton-Earby services as early as the 27th February 1933, but it appears that the actual sale of the 13 Maudslays and one Albion did not occur until the 23rd October of that year, because Ribble Motor Services and West Yorkshire Road Car had notified B.C.N. of their intentions to oppose the application for Laycocks' licences. Ribble were invited to negotiate with the Joint Committee, but apart from stipulating that Ribble stage services could not operate through Colne (although the Manchester-Colne express route was later extended to Skipton), agreement was not reached because Ribble demanded joint running on the former Laycock services. Their interest at this late stage was ironic considering that they had declined the offer to buy Laycock outright. Thus, under opposition lodged by Ribble, West Yorkshire and the London Midland and Scottish Railway, B.C.N. applied for and gained the Laycock operations on the Colne-Keighley, Skipton-Earby and Barnoldswick-Earby routes (the latter under the guise of a new Colne-Earby service), but was refused the two Skipton-Barnoldswick and the Skipton-Bolton Abbey services. From the Minutes of the Joint Committee it appears that Burnley, Colne and Nelson ran in the breach on the three services which had been refused until a deputation was received from Barnoldswick U.D.C. in December 1933, asking for the permanent re-instatement of the Laycock buses. This was agreed and six Maudslays were sold back to Ezra Laycock and Sons at a nominal sum. Another Maudslay and the Albion were withdrawn in April 1934, whilst for some unexplained reason Maudslay ML3 number 38 was finally transferred to B.C.N. in that month.

The Earby-Barnoldswick service ceased on the take-over of Laycocks as B.C.N. decided to delay recommencement until the new road between Salterforth and Kelbrook had been completed. The delay was compounded when negotiations were reopened with Ribble over joint running and it was not reinstated until the 14th November 1934. A co-ordination agreement between Ribble and B.C.N. was finally implemented on 5th March 1935 in the area bounded by Skipton, Colne and Gisburn, whereby both partners were able to effect an operational saving of one vehicle.

B.C.N. numbered the seven ex-Laycock ML3s 64-70 and for two months paid John and Rennie to drive them between Colne and Keighley. From all reports, the Maudslays created a favourable impression with their new owners, their speed and smooth ride being far superior to any of the petrol-engined Leylands which B.C.N. operated. Their strongest feature was the engines, which were fitted with overhead camshafts, a similar layout to that used on the Rover 2000 car today, but Drivers did encounter difficulty with the fierce clutch, which would shriek when not handled correctly. The clutch was rather unusual in that it was conical in shape and leather lined; castor oil, which didn't rot the leather, being added when the gear change became too fierce. Passengers, too, liked the vehicles, the leopard skin seat covers giving journeys a touch of luxury! The last of the seven Maudslays ran with B.C.N. until 1938; 64-69 stayed at Heifer Lane Garage in Colne, but No. 70 moved to Queensgate Depot in Burnley soon after acquisition from Laycocks. This move was probably caused by the purchase by Keighley-West Yorkshire Services (the company formed after an agreement between Keighley Corporation and West Yorkshire, which replaced the Municipal bus fleet in Keighley) of one sixth of the Colne-Keighley route, to give them an equal share of the service with B.C.N., the latter providing two thirds of the buses, following the purchase of the Laycock third. This was effected on the 22nd April 1934, when a new timetable was introduced.

Thus, in December 1933, John and Rennie Laycock regained three stage service licences. Of these, the Skipton-Bolton Abbey route passed to S. & F. Motor Service and the Skipton-Barnoldswick via Thornton service was withdrawn as the sale of the Skipton-Earby licence prevented Laycocks from carrying passengers to Thornton. The third, the Skipton-Barnoldswick via East Marton and West Marton route was, after due consideration by the brothers, continued and therefore, after a break of slightly over a month when the firm had technically ceased to exist, the Laycock business recommenced operations.

The Skipton-Halton East-Bolton Abbey route, as already mentioned, passed to Stephenson and Fotherby trading as S. & F. Motor Service. Mr A. G. Stephenson was the son of W. Stephenson, Ezra Laycock's partner between 1905 and 1912, and together with Mr Fotherby and an ex-employee, Mr Ken Brigg, operated two Maudslay ML4s, which were originally Laycock numbers 20 and 22. These were replaced by more ex-Laycock buses: YG17 and YG19 which had previously been B.C.N. numbers 64 and 66. The former passed to a Mr L. Hutchinson of Skipton in 1938 and was out of service from 1939 until Mr Stephenson rebought it in 1947, when it was rebodied for coaching as the Skipton-Bolton Abbey service had lapsed during the war, being resumed by Ribble in 1946, notionally operating jointly with West Yorkshire. YG19 was downseated from 32 to 26 and was replaced in 1938 by YG18, the third of the batch which was scrapped after only six months with S. & F. The route taken by the service required the driver to turn his vehicle round in Halton East, as there is only one road to the village on which buses can operate. On one occasion, a Bolton Abbey-bound bus, having turned round in the village, returned down the road to Skipton. The driver was unaware of his error until a passenger asked if they were going a long way round to get to Bolton Abbey!

The buses owned by Ezra Laycock and Sons were not the only casualties of the take-over, however, as a small haulage fleet and a private hire car were also sold. The last horses at Cowling were retired, having been retained for use at funerals. The three garages at North Ends, Cowling; Firth Street, Skipton; and Bank Street, Barnoldswick, were disposed of, the latter having superseded the Premier Garage in Earby, became an ambulance depot. They were replaced by a new building in West Close Road, Barnoldswick, which served the business until it was sold for a second and final time in 1972.

Ezra Laycock had always been renowned for employing good men on his buses but, on the sale, they too had to go their separate ways.

Men like Eric Chew, Percy Goad, Ernest Dawson, Herbert Smith, Frank Wiseman, Arthur Overend, the Berry brothers, George Lancaster and his brother, and Ernie Bannister, who married Ezra's daughter, worked all hours of the day for 15s. a week. Ezra would play cards in the hut at Cowling, waiting for a job and when a bus broke down, he would give the driver an ounce of tobacco to repair it. He appointed Walter Snowden as inspector after finding too much money was being pilfered. In typical fashion, he called all his staff together and pronounced: "There's four wheels to a bus and before it was three wheels for Ezra and one wheel for ye buggers, but now it's one wheel for Ezra and three wheels for ye buggers, so I'm making Walter Snowden Inspector to watch after ye all". None of the drivers and conductors ever wore a uniform other than a cap, in stark contrast to the strict regulations of the corporation and company crews of the time. With the exception of the joint service between Colne and Keighley, which was worked by the ML3s, all Laycocks' routes were one-man operated, to keep costs to the minimum.

Unable to reconcile himself to the fact that buses in colours other than his own were operating on his Cowling road, Ezra retired. He moved to the shores of Morecambe Bay where, alert and observant to the last, he died, late in 1933. This book is a tribute to his unceasing service to the South Craven area. He possessed great foresight and the determination to put his pioneering ideas into practice. In his later years, he was frequently known to reflect with a very wry chuckle on the lost freedom of the days when he had to pit his wits against another man's to survive. Through the green buses to which he devoted so much effort, his name will be remembered for many years to come.

From 1933, Ezra Laycock and Sons, the title under which John and Rennie traded, assumed a role similar to any small independent concern operating a rural stage carriage service. To travel on a Laycocks' bus between the cotton town of Barnoldswick and the busy market town of Skipton during the 'thirties was akin to joining a happy family, where everyone knew everyone else on first-name terms. The route itself has always been compared to the Yorkshire equivalent of the Grand National Course at Aintree. The canal was crossed by hump-back bridges no less than four times within two miles of leaving Barnoldswick, at Coates, Greenberfield (twice) and South Field, because in those days the road to Skipton followed Coates Lane to Greenberfield and Greenberfield Lane thence to Ghyll Brow. Allied to these obstacles were several blind right angle bends and the tortuous Marton Lane, with its poor road surface. Fortunately, the drivers were so familiar with its potholes that even at night time passengers were given as smooth a ride as possible. Even so, tributes were frequently made to the drivers' skill at negotiating the numerous obstacles with their unwieldy vehicles.

In 1934 the first of many Bedfords was delivered and numbered 39. Bedford had commenced construction of buses in 1931, at the Vauxhall works in Luton, with a chassis designed for a 14-seat body, later superseded by a vehicle carrying 20 passengers. However, this num-

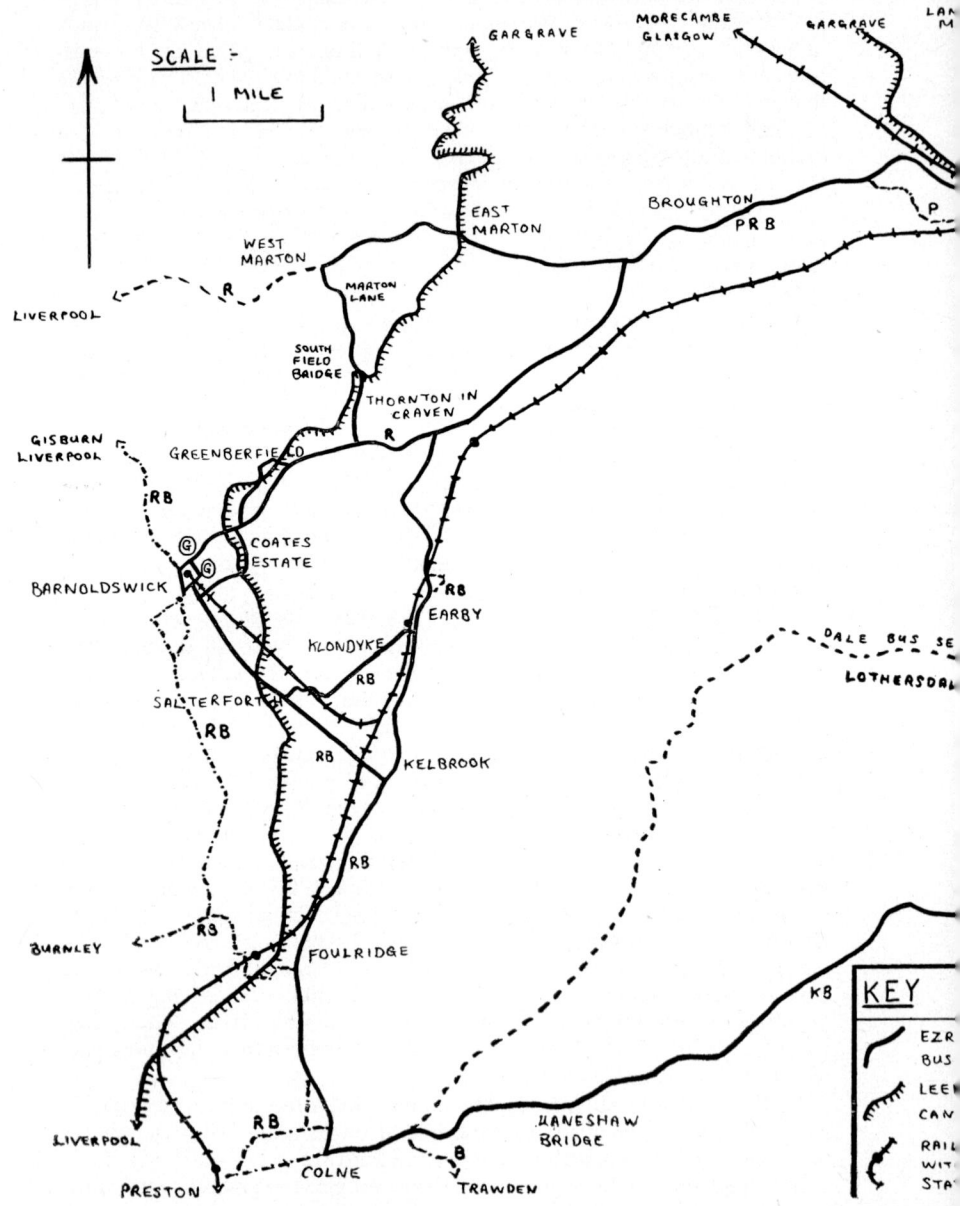

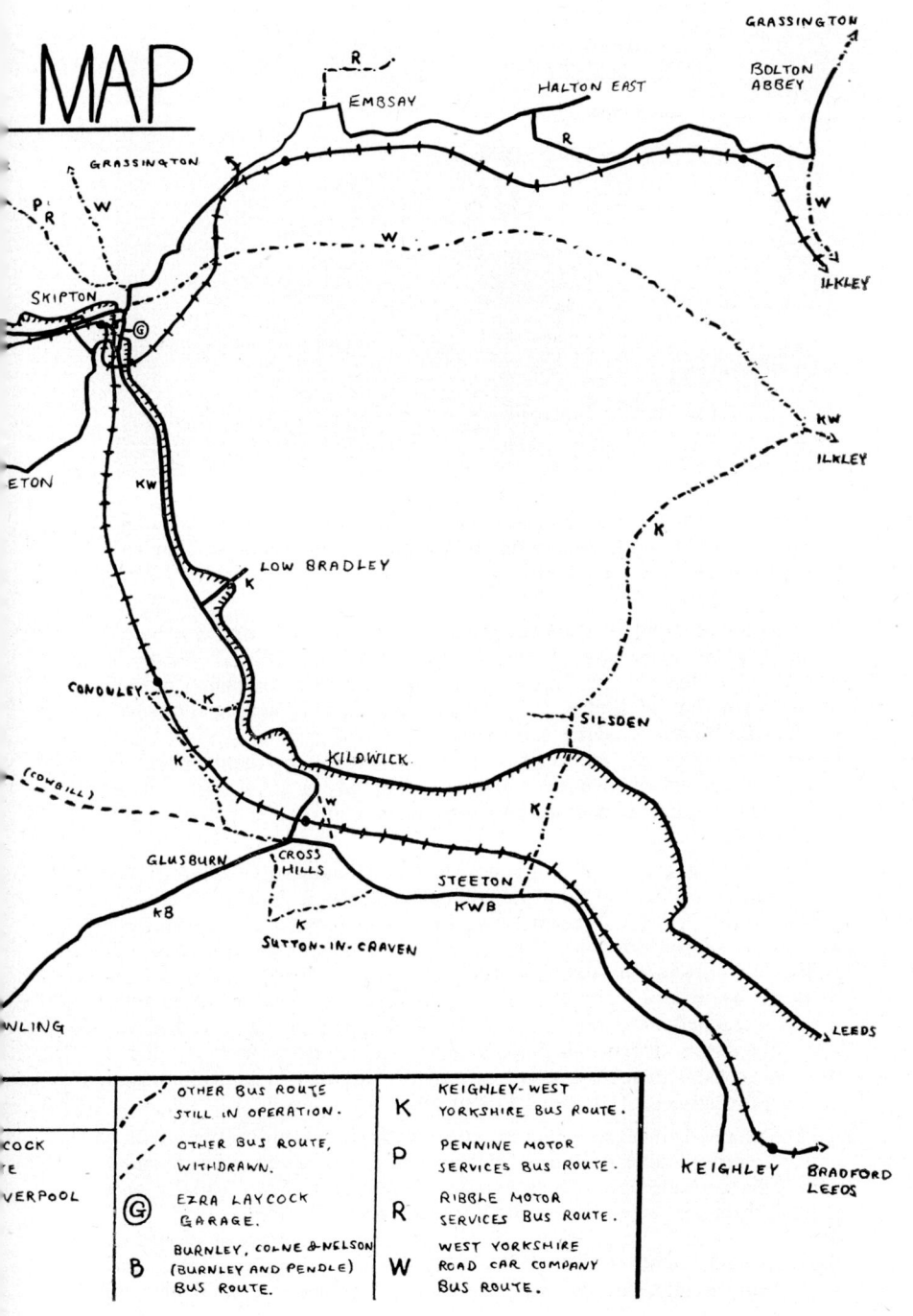

The first Bedford was a 26-seater with a WTL lorry chassis. Although carrying a light load, cornering at Greenberfield Canal Bridge still proved a tricky job for the driver. (Keighley News)

ber was insufficient for Laycocks' needs and their new bus was based on an adapted lorry chassis, designated the WTL. The 26-seat body was built at Hendon by Duple, a firm whose history has been closely linked with that of Bedford. Ever since the late 1930s the Bedford-Duple combination coach has been the most popular cheap lightweight vehicle on the market and, as such, few independent operators can claim never to have operated one. Indeed, in 1939, 70% of all small buses and coaches coming into service in the UK were built by Bedford.

The following year, 1935, a new Bedford chassis appeared in the fleet. This was the WTB, which was specifically a 26-seat passenger service vehicle (P.S.V.) chassis. Number 40, as it became, and number 41, delivered in 1936, were powered by 27 hp Bedford petrol engines, but subsequent vehicles had 28 hp units. The 26-seat coachwork on 41 was built by Barnaby, as were the bodies on 42 and 43, which were delivered in 1937 and 1939, respectively. The latter was a WTB2 which incorporated a new Bedford radiator which was fitted to most of their buses and coaches until 1950 and which is illustrated in the photograph of Bedford OB number 48.

Both sons drove the vehicles, cementing the family spirit which existed in the business. Rennie was always a very quiet, friendly man whilst his brother had a very extrovert character. They usually employed three or four drivers who would work throughout the day, driving to and from Skipton. Buses left the Conservative Club, in Barnoldswick, at 45 minutes past every hour during the week and at 20-minute intervals on Saturdays, with departures at 20 and 40 minutes past and on the hour. The journey took 34 minutes, so that during the turn-round period in Barnoldswick, vehicles had time to make a trip to Coates Estate, when enough new houses had been built there, to justify the re-introduction of the service. The school bus to Skipton left Barnoldswick at 8.15 am. On the return journey, it would stop to pick up Mr N. Wild at his home in Aireview Terrace, Skipton, so that he did not have to catch the earlier 8.45 bus to reach his work in Barnoldswick. The three-month ticket cost £2 12s., but on one occasion, when Mr Wild spent the money, John Laycock loaned it to him!

The other drivers during this time were Ted Cooke, Billy Simpson and Jack Conley, who were later joined by Abe Piper, Joe Lucas, Ray Stapleton and Harold Tomlinson. They would always stop to deliver parcels, or wait for regular customers whom they knew usually caught a particular bus. Frequently, a packed bus would have to wait whilst the driver left his cab to deliver a message, or helped an elderly person, but no-one ever minded as those were leisurely times. However, on occasions, these practices could lead to missed rail connections at Skipton Station. Mrs M. Sharp recalled for me how, when returning to Chesterfield after visiting her grand-parents at Bracewell, the Laycock bus to Skipton halted at nearly every bus stop to pick up ladies going to a meeting. As each boarded, the driver enquired, "Are you going t'Happy How?" The time of the train departure drew near and, in a state of panic, her father, Mr Metcalfe, struggled to the front of the crowded bus to explain the situation to the driver. With no time to spare the train was caught, in spite of the "Happy How"!!

The oldest member of the Laycock staff, Ted Cooke, was a great talker. Regardless of weather conditions, he would always turn round as he was driving to chat with his passengers, even if it was someone he had never seen before. He was always having his leg pulled about this, but was never known to have had an accident. The two buses on the Skipton-Barnoldswick service passed each other at East Marton, but on one foggy night the bus to Skipton met Ted at Broughton. Ted had been talking again and upon reaching Niffney Corner, instead of following the main road on its sharp left hand bend, had driven his vehicle on to the swing bridge over the canal, which leads to the farm.

Falling trees presented another problem where the road to Skipton passes the park of Broughton Hall. On one windy Monday morning, a tree fell at the Broughton Bull, blocking the road in both directions. A queue rapidly formed, stopping the 9.45 to Skipton and several lorries travelling to the auction market. Whilst the bemused drivers pondered the situation, tragedy struck, as another tree was blown down, killing the driver of a cattle truck in his cab. Ironically, the cows escaped unscathed, with the exception of one with a broken horn. Some years later, the driver of the Skipton bus received forewarning of a fallen tree from a car owner who had turned back at the obstacle. After learning that it was down between the two lodges of Broughton Hall, the driver took his vehicle through the grounds.

However, the only exit was over a narrow wooden bridge. All the passengers disembarked and walked across, to await the bus, which crossed with only an inch to spare on either side.

The stage service was not the only side to the business, as the two Laycock brothers were always prepared to undertake private hire work when someone called, either at the garage or at their homes, with a job. During Wake's Weeks they were rushed off their feet, providing excursions for the people of Barnoldswick. John Laycock was a very keen fan of Burnley Football Club and every Saturday, when there was a home fixture, drove a coach-load of supporters to Turf Moor to watch the match. Pendle Hill today is renowned for the witches on Halloween, but during the 1930s it was a favourite haunt for the people of the cotton towns on Good Friday. Every year the Barley Omnibus Company, unable to cope with the crowds, hired two buses from Laycocks. Ezra Laycock and Sons never organised coach tours of their own, but vehicles and their drivers were often hired out to Premier Tours, of Preston. One such venture, in 1937, took John Laycock to Torquay, together with a Barley Omnibus Co. vehicle, driven by Ray Stapleton, who later joined Laycocks as a driver.

The Second World War caused an immediate curtailment of excursions and tours but, unlike the First World War, no vehicles were requisitioned and the firm was allowed to keep its drivers. Sufficient fuel was allocated to the business to maintain the timetable and operate workers' specials. However, the Saturday service was reduced to a 40-minute frequency, the buses leaving Barnoldswick and Skipton at 9.00, 9.40, 10.20 am, etc. Interior lighting was reduced and headlights on the vehicles were masked so that on foggy nights, passengers sometimes had to walk in front of the bus as guides, but in time, the drivers grew to know the route so well that they could even avoid all the pot holes when driving, almost literally blindfold. During the very severe Winter of 1940, one of the buses became stranded in deep snow, near South Field Bridge. When John Laycock returned the following day, it was nowhere to be seen. Indeed, it remained completely buried in the snow for a full week before it could be dug out! Thus, compared with other operators, Laycocks fared well in the War, avoiding cuts in services through bombing and fuel shortages, which caused some companies to convert buses to trailer gas units.

Restrictions on vehicle production did affect them, however. From 1939 to 1942 no motor buses were produced in Britain for the home market, but in the latter year the Ministry of Supply eased its restrictions. 447 chassis which had been built in 1939, or 1940, were "unfrozen" and sent to the body builders. Guy, Daimler, Karrier, Bedford and later Bristol were allowed to build buses for allocation to the areas of greatest need. The bodies were of an austere design, with square wooden construction, devoid of any superfluous panelling. These "utility" vehicles, as they were known, had spartan interiors with wooden bench seats and little or no lighting. The standard livery was grey (to economise in paint and labour in the paint shop) relieved only by black roofs to avoid being spotted by enemy aircraft.

In November 1942, Laycocks took delivery of No. 44. It was a Bedford OWB with a Roe body, seating 32. This was essentially a WTB, with a wheel base lengthened to 14ft 6ins and the 1938-designed 28 hp engine. No. 44 was allocated to serve the cotton mills, but by the time No. 45 was delivered, in 1944, Rolls-Royce Ltd. had established its shadow factory for development of jet engines in Barnoldswick and extra transport was needed to carry the workers, who were recruited from a wide area. The new OWB had a Duple body, identical to that built by Roe on the first vehicle.

The wooden slat seats on 44 and 45 were extremely strong and were never known to break. There were only two lights in the interior, whilst the diminutive headlights gave the absolute minimum of light. They were known to the drivers as the buses with "the elastic sides". Certainly the absence of panelling inside gave a very spacious look to their 7ft 6ins width. During the War, the police always turned a blind eye to the numbers carried on the workers' services, as did all the local Vehicle Examiners, who knew the Laycocks well. Ray Stapleton often drove one of the Rolls-Royce special services, which were operated by two vehicles. However, one evening, the second bus broke down and all the Rolls employees somehow had to reach Skipton. Ray cleverly organised them and when 32 people were seated, another 32 had to sit on their knees. This completed, the remainder stood two abreast in the aisle. Unfortunately, a Traffic Commissioners' Vehicle Examiner from another area happened to be in Skipton when the vehicle arrived and meticulously counted 70 people disembark from the 32-seater! A few days later, a letter was received at the Laycocks' garage, stating that this gross overcrowding had been noted and would they please refrain from this practice in future. Thus, an incident which, under normal conditions, could have led to the Laycock fleet being compulsorily taken off the road, was "overlooked" in the comradeship of wartime.

Unlike the majority of operators, Laycocks did not rush to buy new buses immediately hostilities ended. Their first post-war purchase was delivered in January 1948. Numbered 46, it was a Bedford OB, fitted with luxurious Barnaby 27-seat coachwork. This new chassis appeared in 1939, when 73 were built, before production stopped and the OWB replaced it. The ubiquitous OB reappeared in 1945 as a cheap, reliable 29-seater, with the well-tried 28 hp petrol engine. By the time production ceased, in 1950, 12,693 further examples had been built, making it one of the most popular buses of all time.

Most OBs had Duple bodies, as did Laycocks' number 47, which they bought when a year old, from Kia Ora, of Morecambe, in 1949. The next bus marked a new departure, as it was fitted with a Perkins P6 diesel, or compression ignition (c.i.) engine. This unit had six cylinders, which developed 83 bhp at 2,400 rpm. Although noisier and slower, with much more vibration than a petrol engine, the diesel is far more economical to operate and for this reason was fitted to three of the WTBs in later life, when the coaches were relegated to bus duties. A second diesel-engined Bedford OB was delivered in 1951.

After the war, Certificates of Fitness were refused to all Bedford OWBs which were not reduced in capacity from 32. As a result, both Laycocks' 44 and 45 were downseated to 31, with number 44 later becoming a 30-seater. These vehicles rapidly deteriorated in condition, their ungainly, square war-time lines detracting from the general appearance of the fleet. Number 45 was sold to W. Tetley of Leeds in January 1950, who in turn sold it to the R.A.S.C. in March 1951. They exported it to Egypt where it saw "action" in the 1956 Suez Crisis. 44 was also withdrawn in January 1950, but was deemed suitable for reconstruction. The Hull coach builders of Barnaby re-equipped this vehicle with a Perkins P6 diesel engine and a 31-seat fully-fronted body, modifying the chassis to forward control by moving the driving position next to the engine at the same time. The resulting "new" bus was numbered 50 and registered LWT769 on its return to service in June 1952.

In 1946, the Saturday timetable reverted to its pre-war 20-minute frequency but, in common with all other transport undertakings, the bitter Winter of 1947 caused much disruption on the Skipton-Barnoldswick service. For two months, Marton Lane was almost continuously impassable and buses had to run through Thornton. One day, after a particularly severe blizzard, the Colne-Cross Hills road was blocked and traffic had to travel via Skipton. The last bus through from Barnoldswick left at 1.45 pm and didn't arrive back from Skipton until 7.45 pm — 6 hours to travel 24 miles! The bus, with chains attached to its wheels, had little difficulty, but the passage was hampered by heavy lorries in distress. In particular, a waggon and trailer, which stuck at the Tempest Arms, Elslack, proved immovable, causing long delays whilst a way round was cleared.

During the War, John and Rennie's two sons entered the firm. Roy Laycock was a joiner by trade, whilst Donald, Rennie's son, was an engineer. The early post-war period was a time of rapid expansion in the bus industry, culminating in the record year of 1949, when more buses and coaches were built and passengers carried than ever before and probably ever will be again. However, Ezra Laycock and Sons remained fairly static in size and activity. When John suggested expansion, there was a difference of opinion with his brother, eventually resulting in Rennie and Donald leaving the business. In January 1952, the firm became a limited company, trading as Ezra Laycock Ltd., with its registered office in West Close Road, Barnoldswick, the directors being John and Roy Laycock and Harry Holdsworth, one of the drivers.

May 13th, 1955 was an important date for the firm of Ezra Laycock Ltd., as it marked the Golden Anniversary of the arrival of the original Milnes-Daimler: the "First bus in Yorkshire". Many local newspapers carried articles on the event, an excerpt from one being included in this book. In one interview, when asked the question "What would be, today, the equivalent of your father's first adoption

The post-war derivitive of the WTL was the OB, exemplified by no. 48; one of two bought new by Laycock. On withdrawal it passed to Bolton-by-Bowland Motors. (C. A. L. Wright Collection)

After 8 years' excellent service, petrol-engined utility Bedford OWB no. 43 was reconditioned by Barnaby of Hull in 1952. The resulting rebuild, seen here in Skipton Bus Station, was fitted with a Perkins diesel engine. On withdrawal, this bus also stayed in the West Riding, being sold to Walker of Slaidburn. (C. A. L. Wright Collection)

of motor transport?" John Laycock replied, "We should of course have on order for delivery on the morning of our Golden Jubilee, a multi-seater helicopter, but we prefer a life more tranquil than this might involve".

In 1954, Laycocks' took delivery of the first of two AEC Monocoaches. These machines had their AEC AH410 diesel engines positioned under the floor, at the centre of the bus, and were equipped with five-speed syncromesh gearboxes. Unlike the majority of buses, where the chassis and body are separate and often built by different manufacturers, the Monocoach was one integral unit similar to a motor car, or the latest Leyland National buses of today. The 30-feet long body seated 44 passengers, 12 more than in any previous Laycock single-deck vehicle, and was built by Park Royal Vehicles, a company with a long history of close co-operation with AEC.

Despite the popularity of AEC vehicles, the Monocoach did not sell well outside Scotland, where the state-owned Bus Group bought 189 new and two second-hand from a small independent concern. Thus, Laycock numbers 51 and 52, which came in 1956, were probably the only Monocoaches bought new by an English independent.

The reason for this lack of appeal was probably the popularity of AEC's other single-deck chassis at that time, the Reliance. Although heavier and a little more expensive than its stablemate, the Reliance offered the more powerful AH470 engine and an unlimited choice of bodywork to be fitted, making it popular with operators who have always had favourite coach builders. Ezra Laycock No. 53, delivered in March 1959, was a Reliance with a 43-seater body, built by Charles H. Roe of Leeds, which was later altered to carry 45 seats. During the same year, a secondhand AEC Regal III was bought from Cowgill (Dales Bus Service) of Lothersdale.

This short-lived Regal was superseded in 1960 by another, also from a local source — Wild Bros. of Barnoldswick. This amazing coach had originated as Bath Tramways number 2219, in 1937, and had passed to Wild via Berresford of Cheddleton on withdrawal in 1951. They despatched their acquisition to the coachworks of Yeates, in Loughborough, who lengthened the chassis to 30 feet and fitted a new AEC diesel engine and 37-seat body. In this form LWX888 (its new registration) carried the chassis number of WSY/06622310/189 — possibly the longest ever used on a bus.

1960 also saw the return of Bedfords to the fleet, in the form of 56 and 57. These were SB1s, with 41-seat Duple coach bodies. This chassis, which replaced the OB, was introduced in 1950 and by 1965, when it went into limited production (as it still is today), had sold over 14,000 chassis — a United Kingdom record. In an effort to give the firm of Ezra Laycock a new image, number 56 was painted in a light blue livery and 57 dark blue, but as neither was successful, the dark green livery lived on.

The next major date in the Company's life was August 1961, when J. T. Hey, trading as Silver Star Motor Services, was taken over, with

An unusual vehicle was this integral AEC/Park Royal Vehicles Monocoach which was of chassis-less construction. Number 51 was the first of two bought by Ezra Laycock Ltd. and is seen in Skipton Bus Station in 1955 when less than a year old.
(C. A. L. Wright Collection)

The most numerous AEC single-decker of the 1950s was the Reliance which could be bodied by the manufacturer of the operator's choice. In the case of Laycocks' 53, Park Royal's associate Company of C. H. Roe constructed the coachwork.   (C. A. L. Wright Collection)

the Skipton-Carleton stage service and a workers' special between Carleton and a mill in Broughton Road, Skipton. The three Bedfords which Silver Star owned were operated by Laycocks for two weeks before being sold. All were OBs, JWW933 being bought new by Mr Hey, whilst the diesel-engined GOU721 came from Hants and Sussex Motor Service. None was numbered by Laycocks, during their short stay. Silver Star also operated a Skipton-Bradley route which, on acquisition, Laycocks allowed to lapse until Keighley-West Yorkshire diverted their route 8 (Skipton-Silsden) through the village. It is interesting to note that a blind, including the Bradley destination removed from one of the Bedfords, was carried by Bristol No. 84, as late as 1972. The return journeys on the new route were fitted into the waiting time of buses at Skipton on the Barnoldswick service, with one vehicle spending the night behind a public house in Carleton.

Replacements for the ex-Silver Star buses were quickly sought and arrived in the form of two AEC Regals from Trent, a Leyland from Ribble and a Tilling-Steven. The Leyland was already 26 years old when purchased, having started life as a service bus. In 1950 it was rebodied as a coach and given a Leyland E181 engine, a unit which had been designed for use in Second World War tanks. Many similar vehicles were sold to independent operators around 1960, one of which, belonging to Progress of Chorley, lasted until 1973, when it was estimated to have run three million miles in its 38 years service. However, neither Laycocks' number 60, nor 61, the Tilling, lasted long, the latter being sold after the engine blew up. A Ford Thames demonstrator, 8608EV, was also hired for a few weeks in 1961 for use on the Carleton service.

Numbers 62 and 63 were AEC Reliances, with Duple Britannia 41-seat coachwork. These smart vehicles were the last to be bought new by Laycocks until 1972, demonstrating the catastrophic effect the private car was having on the bus industry. In order to pay for the new AECs, the two Bedford SB1s and an AEC Monocoach had to be sold. Two more secondhand AECs were acquired in 1962. The first, numbered 66, was a Regal III chassis which, following the advent of underfloor-engined vehicles, had ceased to be built for the home market between 1954 and the appearance of this machine in 1959. Number 67, though five years older, was of the more advanced Reliance model, but the body, built to coach standards, proved unsuitable for stage service and it was exchanged in December 1962 for a new number 67. The Ford demonstrator hired in 1961 had obviously created a good impression, as 1456PT was a Thames Trader with a Willowbrook service body, rather rare on a chassis marketed primarily as a coach. Both 66 and the second 67 passed for further service when sold by Laycocks, the Regal now working in Ireland.

Double-deckers had not been operated by Ezra Laycock since the middle 1920s, so the arrival of number 70, in 1964, caused considerable interest. School children living in Barnoldswick had always used the railway to reach Skipton, but it was decided to hire a bus because of the impending closure of Barnoldswick Station. Thus, the 54-seat Leyland PD1, HCD903 was bought from Southdown Motor Services,

Three elderly Bedford OBs taken-over with the Silver Star business were soon withdrawn by Ezra Laycock. However, amongst the replacements was this even older Leyland Tiger which was acquired after 26 years with Ribble. No. 60 is photographed leaving Skipton on the former Silver Star route to Carleton.
(C. A. L. Wright Collection)

ODE 777 seen when working for Mosley of Barugh Green before sale to Laycock. This rare machine was a Tilling-Stevens Express with a Meadows engine and a Brush body built on a Duple "6" frame.
(C. A. L. Wright Collection)

66 (RKU 221) was one of the last AEC Regal IIIs to be built. Its full-front Plaxton body seated 39. (C. A. L. Wright Collection)

The second number 67, an ex-Trimdon Motor Services Ford Thames with Duple Midland bodywork replaced the original 67, an elderly AEC Reliance. (C. A. L. Wright Collection)

Ex-Devon General Leyland "Royal Tiger" with Willowbrook bodywork, is seen parked at Salterforth when withdrawn by Laycocks.
(C. A. L. Wright Collection)

In order to keep apace with competitors in the private-hire field, Laycocks bought two of these AEC Reliances with Duple Britannia coachwork in 1962. (C. A. L. Wright Collection)

who had run it since new in 1947. This bus was stabled for the night in the paint shop, the main garage being too low to accommodate it. On arrival in Skipton, it spent the day parked in the centre of the bus station, between setting down and picking up at Ermysteds and the High School.

At the commencement of the next school year, in September 1965, two AEC Regent III double-deckers were purchased from Western S.M.T., who had bought them new in 1950. Their early demise was probably because they were non-standard in that Scottish fleet where Leyland, Bristol, Daimler and Guy machines predominated. These vehicles, although of low-bridge construction (i.e. the upper deck gangway was sunken at the side, allowing an overall height of 13ft 6ins — 9ins lower than a conventional vehicle) still proved too high to be accommodated in the main garage and, as a result, when not in Skipton were usually to be found parked outside the paint shop, which could only accommodate one vehicle.

The double-deckers were operated without conductors, so that the school children were unsupervised. A favourite prank of theirs was to hang off the back of the open platform at the rear, causing great concern to motorists behind the bus. Realising that the situation could not be tolerated, three new double-deckers, with platform doors, were bought. These were numbered 74-76, having originated with Ribble, as its 2494, 2485 and 2509 respectively. This batch, built in 1947, had comprised 38 buses, all fitted with Brush 53-seat bodies. Subsequently, 16 were sold and the remainder rebodied in 1955 by H. V. Burlingham, in Blackpool, to similar capacities and converted to 8ft wide, their E181 engines being replaced by 0.600 units, four years later.

From 1966 to 1968, three secondhand AEC Reliances were purchased. The first, number 77, was burnt out a year after it arrived. Although thoughts were given to reconstruction, they never came to fruition and it was replaced by 78. This machine carried a smart Plaxton Highway body which wasn't displayed to its best advantage by the application of the Laycock livery. In later years, it was re-seated to carry 45, as a service bus. Number 79, however, was very ungainly in appearance and only stayed a year before being re-sold.

In 1968, sufficient school children were carried to warrant the purchase of a fourth double-decker. Again this was an ex-Ribble Leyland, but being more modern, lacked the complicated history of the other three. However, despite the income this side of the business generated, the coach fleet of AECs was becoming rather elderly in appearance and newer vehicles were needed. Against the advice of his mechanic, Mr Laycock bought a 1966 Ford, with Plaxton 45-seat coachwork. This vehicle, which became number 81, frequently worked on the Rolls-Royce service, in conjunction with a normal bus. The bus always ran to Skipton direct, whilst the coach operated via Barnoldswick, but despite the simplicity of the system, there was quite often some confusion. The Ford was also hired to Wild Bros. from time to time, for use on the contract to Johnson and Johnson at Gargrave.

The first double-deckers to be owned for over 40 years were these secondhand vehicles. 72 and 73 were lowbridge AEC Regent IIIs, bought from Western S.M.T., whilst 70 was a highbridge Leyland PD1 which originated with Southdown. All three are seen parked on waste ground near Waller Hill Bus Station in Skipton, awaiting the closure of local schools. (C. A. L. Wright Collection)

One of three Leyland PD1As which replaced the vehicles in the above photograph, 75 was extensively rebuilt by Ribble when only 8 years old. (C. A. L. Wright Collection)

This Plaxton bodied AEC Reliance passed third-hand to Laycock but was in constant use until it was sold in the AEC replacement programme. (C. A. L. Wright Collection)

The low height, designed to avoid such calamities, did not prevent number 75 from colliding with a bridge in Nelson, during 1969. Because of its age, the decision was taken to scrap it and a replacement was bought. This materialised as a 1958 AEC Regent V, which was 30 feet in length, accommodating 65 passengers in considerable comfort, as this type usually seats eight more. Laycocks fitted platform doors, though it ran in the attractive red, black and cream colours of its former owner, City of Oxford Motor Services, for some time afterwards. When it was repainted, the number was missing, a point brought to Mr Laycock's attention by a keen-eyed enthusiast.

Experimenting with different manufacturers continued with the arrival of No. 84, a 1955 Bristol LS5, from West Yorkshire Road Car Co. This was an integral vehicle, produced for the nationalised British Transport Holdings, which had bought out the Tilling Group in 1947. The body was an Eastern Coach Works 41-seater, to dual purpose standards, i.e. coach seating in a bus frame. The Gardner 5LW engine, whilst being slow, was one of the finest diesel units in the world. This design was first announced in 1928 and the six-cylinder 6LW is still being produced today. The 5LW produces 85 bhp at 1,700 rpm from its 7 litres capacity and, well maintained, can achieve 15 miles to the gallon. This performance was in marked contrast to that achieved by the AEC Reliances, which were encountering increasing gasket trouble, a fault common in their AH470 engines.

The first Bristol LS5G, no. 84, was bought from West Yorkshire Road Car and proved so successful in terms of reliability and low fuel consumption that two more followed from West Yorkshire together with three from Bristol. (C. A. L. Wright Collection)

Unlike the semi-coach standards which the ex-West Yorkshire Bristols originally set, no. 89 was a normal service bus, as can be seen in this view taken in the Barnoldswick depot yard.
(C. A. L. Wright Collection)

Following the success of number 84, two more LS5Gs were acquired, this time from the Bristol Omnibus Company's subsidiary, Bath Tramways. They operated for several weeks in their former owner's green livery, with the existing advertisements and without blinds, which caused much confusion. Ezra Laycock had used advertisements as a useful source of revenue for several years, many local businesses taking advantage of the space on the backs of buses to publicise their goods and services.

Early in 1971, two Bedfords were bought from Shirley, of Meriden, having originated with Gardiner, of Spennymoor, Co. Durham. These 1968 coaches seated 53 passengers in their 36 feet long bodies. This was six feet longer than any previous Laycock vehicle and ten feet longer than the permitted maximum length when the West Close Road Depot was built. Fortunately, the foresight of the builders was repaid as the new coaches fitted neatly into the garage. They were never painted in true Laycock livery, the darker green being so smart that it was considered adopting it as standard, but this plan never came to fruition. Another interesting point about these vehicles was their three axles and small wheels. This gave the VAL70, as they were designated, added stability and safety. Amongst the AEC Reliances which were replaced was number 58, which had also hailed from Gardiners, 11 years before. This coach was sold to a Bradford firm, for use on the Bradford-Pakistan Express. Apparently it performed well, though as happens to most old coaches which traverse the Khyber Pass in each direction, returned home to the scrap heap.

Three more Bristol LS5Gs were bought and numbered 89, 94 and 95 (the latter being the highest-numbered Laycock bus) replacing the remaining AEC Reliances. Leyland double-deck No. 76 was also withdrawn after its engine had blown up. The gap in the numbering was left for four new coaches and, in due course, three new Bedford YRQs were delivered, their Plaxton 45-seat bodies including such extras as forced-air ventilation and specially wide doors. This feature enabled the vehicles to qualify for a 50% grant from the Government, with the added condition that half the work undertaken by them in the first five years of operation must be on stage service carriage. This concession has helped numerous small firms, some of which have bought their first new vehicles since the early 1930s. In April 1972, a magnificent 53-seat Leyland Leopard coach was delivered, which also qualified for a 50% reduction of the £13,500 cost. This bus, number 93, proved to be the last vehicle to be bought. It is unusual that in an area dominated by Leyland buses and coaches, this was only the second vehicle to be bought new from that manufacturer. This coach, together with the three new Bedfords replaced the two VAL70s and the Ford and entered service on the Barnoldswick-Skipton route. This was now possible, as construction of a new road from Coates to Ghyll Brow, in 1958, alleviated the necessity of negotiating the narrow, tortuous roads around Greenberfield.

During the Summer of 1972, it was announced that the company of Ezra Laycock Ltd. had been sold to Pennine Motor Services of

Gargrave, the exact time of the transfer being fixed as midnight on the 11th of August. As this date approached, the garage in Barnoldswick was visited by numerous enthusiasts, anxious for a last photograph or a last ride. On the Wednesday of the final week, an auction of tickets and general bric-à-brac was held in the garage, with a good response from the public. Amongst mementos sold were parts from the AEC Monocoach No. 52, which was dismantled by Laycocks. The fateful Friday arrived and a large crowd gathered as the departure time for the last bus drew near. The vehicle chosen to perform this duty was Leyland Leopard number 93 and, as it drew into the depot, the last passenger disembarked and the last photograph taken, an era drew to a close.

In the later years of operation, even this friendly service suffered a loss of some of the familiarity that existed in former years. However, the drivers and conductors were always willing to share a chuckle and a "chinwag" with their passengers. Amusing incidents never ceased to happen, one of the most audacious occurring at West Marton. Here Marton Lane makes a long detour around Marton Hall Farm, whilst a track through the farmyard is perfectly straight. One day a driver, seeing that the gates at either end were open, decided to save time and diesel oil by taking the short cut.

The new operator altered the Skipton-Barnoldswick route considerably, diverting it to include Carleton, whilst Saturday frequencies were reduced. Only the four new coaches in the Laycock fleet were retained and painted in Pennine's attractive amber and black livery, which was modified to include a green fleet name and some white relief. The double-deckers were sold soon after the take-over, the AEC Regent V passing to Wild Bros. of Barnoldswick. The Bristol LS5Gs, after spending several weeks out of service parked outside the garage, were sold to operators in Lancashire, Scotland and Wales. The school services are now operated by Terry's Taxis, whose two-tone blue AECs, bought from Halifax, now make regular appearances in Skipton and Barnoldswick. Thus, Barnoldswick Depot has become a dormy shed for the two 1971 Leyland Leopard service buses used on the route to Skipton. The paint shop was sold, becoming a private garage, whilst Border Tours (Kellet) coaches are often parked in the depot yard and two preserved Leyland Royal Tigers are housed inside.

Fares had increased considerably since those halcyon days of 1908 when Laycock and Stephenson purchased 1,000 gallons of petrol at 7d (3p) per gallon, delivered free of charge, from London. Even in 1929, when taxes were levied, it only cost 1s 4½d (7p) per gallon, falling to 9d (4p) two years later — a sobering thought in the days of the impending £1 gallon. During the later years, the Skipton-Barnoldswick service was operated at a considerable loss, having to be cross-subsidised from other areas of the business, despite Government aid in tax rebates and grants. Amongst the smaller services performed by the company was the daily carriage of the local evening papers to Barnoldswick, for delivery to the townsfolk. Thus, it is gratifying to note the letters of thanks from his former customers that Mr Laycock received upon his retirement from the business.

It is ironic that plans were being made by the company for many years into the future. More second-hand Bristols were to be bought when those in service became redundant, whilst the double-deck fleet was to be equipped with 70-seaters, which were being withdrawn by large operators at the time. However, the green buses are now a fading memory, with the exception of Leyland double-decker number 74, which was saved for preservation by some Blackburn enthusiasts. When withdrawn from service, it was 25 years years old, making it one of the oldest working Public Service Vehicles in Yorkshire. Although it now carries the livery of Ribble Motor Services, the appearance of BCK437 at rallies throughout the country will serve as a living reminder of Ezra Laycock.

With the sale of the business, Roy Laycock, his wife and daughters, who acted as secretaries to the Company, are now able to devote their entire energies to their farm in Barnoldswick. Some long-serving employees retired, whilst five now work for Pennine.

John Laycock died a few years before the take-over. He was known throughout the Craven area as a character, in the best sense of the word. A stalwart Conservative, he served as president of the Barnoldswick Club for many years and was a regular visitor to the time of his death, always enjoying a friendly game of cards or dominoes. Amongst his greatest loves was motoring. He possessed a large collection of badges which proudly decorated the front of his car. His knowledgeable enthusiasm for motor transport combined with this extrovert nature made conversation with him a pleasure. The motor era and his own business developed as contemporaries from their infancy to modernity in Mr Laycock's life time.

As from 12th August, 1972, the business of Ezra Laycock Ltd. will be taken over by Pennine Motor Services, Gargrave.

Enquiries & Time Tables:
Apply Grouse Garage, Gargrave. Telephone Gargrave 215

One of the two 1971 Leyland Leopards with Willowbrook bodywork which Pennine uses on the Skipton–Carleton–West Marton–Barnoldswick route. (C. A. L. Wright Collection)

FLEET LIST

Reg. No.	Fleet No.	Chassis	Chassis No.	Body & No.	Seating	Year New
AK 335	—	Milnes-Daimler 30 hp			B18R	1905
AK 343	—	Milnes-Daimler 30 hp			025/24ROS	1906
	—	Belsize London Taxi			Taxi	
	—	Belsize London Taxi			Taxi	
AK 3113	—	Maudslay			ch32-	1908
	—				025/25ROS	
	—	Maudslay			C32-	1919
WR 1622	—	Commer n.c. Chain-Drive	5278		025/25ROS	1919
WR 1623	—	Leyland SG5	10047		ch32-	1919
WR 5436	—	Commer 3P Bevel-Drive	10006		B32F	1921
	—	Lancia			ch20-	
	—	Daimler Y			C-	
	—	Belsize 15 hp			Taxi	
	—	Ford T			ch-	
	—	Bean			ch-	
TC 62	—	W. & G. Du Cros Talbot			ch24-	
WT 6718	—	Reo Speedwagon	105659		B14F	1924
	—	Austin 22 hp			Taxi	1924
	16	Morris			Taxi	1925
	17	Standard 6-cylinder			Taxi	1925
WU 3221	18	Maudslay ML4/26	3779	ex-Wright Bros., Burnley	B26F	1925
WU 7124	19	Maudslay ML4/26	3967	,, ,, ,,	B26F	1926
WU 7125	20	Maudslay ML4/26	3969	,, ,, ,,	B26F	1926
WU 9269	21	Maudslay ML4/26	4041	Buckingham	B26F	1927
WU 9268	22	Maudslay ML4/26	4036	Buckingham	B26F	1927
WW 3877	23	Maudslay ML4/26	4207		B26F	1927
WW 5131	24	Maudslay ML3/35	4218		B32F	1928
WW 5132	25	Maudslay ML3/35	4225		B32F	1928
WW 5270	26	Dennis G	(?) 70162		B20F	1928
WW 5271	27	Dennis G	70134		B20F	1928
WW 6110	28	Dennis G	70021		B20F	1928
WW 6111	29	Maudslay ML4/26	4371		ch26-	1928
WW 8139	30	Albion PFB26	4318C	Barnaby	B20-	1928
WW 9068	31	Maudslay ML3/35	4462	Barton & Danson	B32D	1929
WX 325	32	Maudslay ML6/30	4661	Lond. Lorries Ltd	ch26-	1929
WX 3029	33	Maudslay ML3B/35	4836	Barnaby	B32F	1930
WX 3264	34	Commer 23GN	23005	,,	B20F	1930
WX 3266	35	Commer 23GN	23006	,,	B20F	1930
YG 17	36	Maudslay ML3/35	5017	,,	B32F	1932
YG 18	37	Maudslay ML3/35	5054	,,	B32F	1932
YG 19	38	Maudslay ML3/35	5032	,,	B32F	1932
AWR 97	39	Bedford WTL	874607	Duple (48189)	B26F	1935
AWY 26	40	Bedford WTB	110298		B26F	1936
BWR 960	41	Bedford WTB	110790	Barnaby	C26F	1936
CWR 702	42	Bedford WTB	111751	,,	B26F	1937

Into Service	Withdrawn	Purchased from	Sold to	Notes
5/05	/22	New		Rebodied by Laycock (C25F) in 1905
2/06	/20	New	Operator in Skipton area	
	c/24			
	c/24			
/08	/14	New	War Department	
c/10	/14	Lon. Gen. O'bus Co.	War Department	
/19	by/28	New		
/19	by/28	New		May have been a 30-seat s/d until 4/23
/19	by/28	New	Shiels, Magheira, Ireland	
1/21	by/28	New	Wyatt, Northerton, Worcs. (Showmen)	
	by/28			)
	by/28			)
	by/28	New		) All sold by 1928. It is not
	by/28	New		) known whether these are in
	by/28			) the correct chronological
/24	by/28			) order
9/24	by/28	New		
/24	/29	New		
/25	/33	New		
/25	/33	New		
10/25	2/36	New		Rebodied (Knape B24F) from a Claremont McCurd
6/26	2/35	New		Rebodied by body from a Wright Bros. Leyland
6/26	2/35	New	Stephenson & Fotherby, Skipton	Rebodied (Knape B24F) from a Claremont McCurd
1/27	11/37	New	Corner, Barnoldswick, for scrap	Rebodied by Bellhouse-Hartwell (C26F)
1/27	by/35	New	Stephenson & Fotherby, Skipton	Rebodied (Knape B24F) from a Claremont McCurd
10/27	9/36	New		
5/28	10/33	New	Burnley, Colne & Nelson 68	
3/28	10/33	New	Burnley, Colne & Nelson 69	
3/28	2/30	Premier, Earby	Union Jack, Luton	Acquired with Union Jack by Luton Corp. in 1933
3/28	3/30	Premier, Earby	Union Jack, Luton	,, ,, ,, ,,
5/28	/32	New	Maudslay Motors	Ordered by Premier, Earby
5/28	11/28	New	Mitton, Colne	
12/28	1/34	New	Hey, Keighley	
3/29	10/33	New	Burnley, Colne & Nelson 67	Barton & Danson were coachbuilders at Orrel
5/29	3/34	New	Wild Bros., Barnoldswick	Was altered to ch25– in 11/31
2/30	10/33	New	Burnley, Colne & Nelson 70	Later with Wetton, Brimington
3/30	7/32	New	Round, Long Law Ford	
2/30	2/33	New	Roes, West Ham	
3/32	10/33	New	Burnley, Colne & Nelson 64	Later with Stephenson & Fotherby, Skipton
3/32	10/33	New	Burnley, Colne & Nelson 65	,, ,, ,, ,,
5/32	4/34	New	Burnley, Colne & Nelson 66	,, ,, ,, ,,
4/35	10/39	New	Hey, Carleton (Silver Star)	
2/36	12/49	New	Meashams Motor Sales	Fitted with a Perkins P6 engine post-war
8/36	2/46	New	Pickerill, Low Valley	
12/37	5/48	New	Hutchison, Keighley	Fitted with a Perkins P6 engine post-war

FLEET LIST

Reg. No.	Fleet No.	Chassis	Chassis No.	Body & No.	Seating	Year New
DWW 334	43	Bedford WTB2		Barnaby	C26F	1939
EWR 574	44	Bedford OWB	10640	Roe (GO919)	UB32F	1942
EWU 432	45	Bedford OWB	18275	Duple (38694)	UB32F	1944
GWU 653	46	Bedford OB	58390	Barnaby	C27F	1948
JTD 840	47	Bedford OB	79055	Duple (50247)	C29F	1948
JWT 24	48	Bedford OB P6	122768	Mulliner (T548)	B30F	1949
KWR 450	49	Bedford OB P6	68232	Barnaby	B30F	1950
LWT 769	50	Bedford OWB Rebuilt P6	310285	,,	FB31F	1952
CHG 248	51	AEC Monocoach	MC3RV054	Park Royal (37333)	B44F	1954
DHG 654	52	AEC Monocoach	MC3RV143	Park Royal (37046)	B44F	1956
WYG 540	53	AEC Reliance	MU3RV111	Roe	B43F	1959
GYG 803	54	AEC Regal III	9621A464	Burlingham (3578)	FC33F	1948
LWX 888	55	AEC Regal	WSY/06622310/189	Yeates (299)	FC37F	1953
4727 WW	56	Bedford SB1	83076	Duple (1120/500)	C41F	1960
6889 WW	57	Bedford SB1	83219	Duple (1120/547)	C41F	1960
347 BUP	58	AEC Reliance	2MU3RA986	Plaxton (592493)	C41F	1959
MUB 435	—	AEC Regal III	9621E816	Plaxton (2065)	FC35F	1949
KUB 695	59	Daimler CVD6	13275	Roe	B35F	1947
JWW 933	—	Bedford OB	132120	Mulliner (AL9)	C30F	1950
GOU 721	—	Bedford OB P6	94672	Duple (47887)	B30F	1948
SMY 916	—	Bedford OB P6	74056	Duple (44007)	C29F	1948
FV 5734	60	Leyland 'Tiger' TS7	6685	Duple (53838)	C31F	1935
ODE 777	61	TSM L4MA8	9946	Duple (119/11)	FB39F	1952
5496 YG	62	AEC Reliance	2MU3RA3559	Duple (1137/38)	C41F	1961
5497 YG	63	AEC Reliance	2MU3RA3560	Duple (1137/41)	C41F	1961
BRC 308	64	AEC Regal III	6821X438	Willowbrook (50734)	DP33F	1950
BRC 318	65	AEC Regal III	6821X446	,, (50744)	DP33F	1950
RKU 221	66	AEC Regal III	6821A761	Plaxton (592360)	FB39F	1959
CEF 135	67	AEC Reliance	MU3RV429	Plaxton (2705)	C41F	1954
1456 PT	67	Ford 570E	510E53115	Duple Midland (497/42/F10)	B40F	1961
MTT 638	68	Leyland 'Royal Tiger' PSU1/9	502624	Willowbrook (50830)	B43F	1951
UHO 3	69	AEC Reliance	2MU2RA2116	Harrington (2049)	C41F	1958
HCD 903	70	Leyland 'Titan' PD1	470955	Leyland	H28/26R	1947
LVA 269	71	AEC Reliance	MU3RV433	Burlingham (6007)	C41F	1955
BCS 453	72	AEC Regent III	9612E1621	N.C.M.E. (4483)	L27/26R	1950
BSD 442	73	AEC Regent III	9612E1623	N.C.M.E. (4156)	L27/26R	1950
BCK 437	74	Leyland 'Titan' PD1A	470113	Burlingham (5977)	L27/26RD8	1947
BCK 428	75	Leyland 'Titan' PD1A	462225	Burlingham (5979)	L27/26RD8	1947
BCK 452	76	Leyland 'Titan' PD1A	470514	Burlingham (5970)	L27/26RD8	1947
716 AVA	77	AEC Reliance	2MU3RV3062	Duple (1137/3)	C41F	1961
201 AOU	78	AEC Reliance	2MU3RA3217	Plaxton (602333)	DP43F	1960

Into Service	Withdrawn	Purchased from	Sold to	Notes
/39	11/53	New		Fitted with a Perkins P6 engine post-war
11/42	1/50	New	Rebuilt as 50	Was downseated to 31 & 30
/44	1/50	New	W. Tetley, Leeds	Was downseated to 31
1/48	4/56	New	Mobile Shop, Workington	
9/49	4/59	Kia Ora, Morecambe	Rodgers, Redcar	
2/50	12/54	New	Bolton-by-Bowland MS, Clitheroe	
2/51	9/58	New	Hillcrest, Settle	
6/52	3/59	New	Walker, Slaidburn	Rebuilt from no. 44
10/54	2/61	New	Llynfi, Maesteg 80	
1/56	11/69	New	Scrapped by Laycock	
3/59	11/71	New	Macrae, Fortrose	Reseated as B45F in 1970
/59	7/60	Cowgill, Lothersdale	Grant, South Shields	
2/60	7/60	Wild, Barnoldswick	Burgess, Scarborough	Originally Bristol OC 2219 (GL5057)
6/60	3/62	New	Bingley, Kinsley (United)	Painted in a light blue livery
6/60	3/62	New	Bingley, Kinsley (United)	Painted in a dark blue livery
12/60	12/70	Gardiner, Spennymoor	S. Hughes (dealer) Gomersall	Later with Shaheen, Bradford
1/61	3/61	Pashley, Wakefield	Hall, Trelyn	Hired from S. Hughes (dealer) Gomersall
3/61	3/62	Farsley Omnibus Co., Stanningley	Johnstone (Contractor), Garforth	
8/61	8/61	Hey (Silver Star MS) Skipton		Operated for 2 weeks by Laycocks
8/61	8/61	,, ,, ,, ,,		,, ,, ,, ,,
8/61	8/61	,, ,, ,, ,,		,, ,, ,, ,,
8/61	5/63	Ribble MS 752	Blake, Didcot (non PSV)	Body built in 1950
8/61	3/62	Mosley, Barugh Gn.	Hillcrest, Settle	Body built by Brush on Duple shell
11/61	12/70	New	Pirrelli, Warrington (non PSV)	
11/61	12/70	New Trent Motor Traction 108	,, ,, ,,	
11/61	10/62	Trent Motor Traction 108	Metcalfe, Hawes	
11/61	10/62	Trent Motor Traction 118	Grange, Yeadon	
8/62	5/70	Rhind, Wakefield	Gilbert, Salterforth Quarry	Later exported to Ireland
8/62	12/62	Ward, Lepton	Evans, New Tredegar	
12/62	4/64	Trimdon MS	Williams, Scunthorpe	Cameria Pepper, Thurnscoe who hired it
8/63	8/65	Devon Gen. SL638	Scrapped by Laycock	
4/64	1/72	Starr, N. Anston	Black Prince, Leeds	
8/64	9/66	Southdown MS 303	Cowley (dealer) Salford	To Cubbins, Farnworth in 12/66
4/65	1/67	Sykes, Warrington	Millburn Motors, Preston	
9/65	9/66	Western SMT 548	Martin (dealer) Weaverham	
9/65	8/66	Western SMT 584	Cowley (dealer) Salford	To Cubbins, Farnworth in 12/66
7/66	6/72	Ribble MS 2494	Pennine MS (not run)	) Rebuilt in 1955 by Ribble
7/66	10/69	Ribble MS 2485		) when Burlingham replaced) Brush unit with their own
7/66	5/72	Ribble MS 2509		) 8ft wide bodies, 0600 engines) in 1959
12/66	12/67	Hutchison, Overton	Scrapped by Laycock	Burnt out in 12/67
12/67	11/71	Super, Upminster	King, Kirkcowan	Reseated as B45F in 1970

FLEET LIST

Reg. No.	Fleet No.	Chassis	Chassis No.	Body & No.	Seating	Year New
PCJ 533	79	AEC Reliance	MU3RV1635	Duple Midland (483/4)	C41F	1957
ECK 927	80	Leyland 'Titan' PD2/12	52186	Leyland	L27/26RD	1952
CMJ 504D	81	Ford R192	BC01E436338	Plaxton (652734)	C45F	1966
YDK 589	82	AEC Reliance	3565	Harrington	C37F	1961
968 CWL	83	AEC Regent V	425	M.C.C.W.	H37/28R	1958
OWX 144	84	Bristol LS5G	107063	E.C.W.	DP41F	1955
XHW 408	85	Bristol LS5G	117128	E.C.W.	B45F	1956
XHW 409	86	Bristol LS5G	117129	E.C.W.	B45F	1956
AUP 402F	87	Bedford VAL70	454303	Duple Northern	C53F	1968
AUP 403F	88	Bedford VAL70	444327	Duple Northern	C53F	1968
XHW 401	89	Bristol LS5G	117108	E.C.W.	B45F	1956
MYG 759K	90	Bedford YRQ	471610	Plaxton	C45F	1972
MYG 760K	91	Bedford YRQ	471811	Plaxton	C45F	1972
MYG 761K	92	Bedford YRQ	471718	Plaxton	C45F	1972
OWY 179K	93	Leyland 'Leopard' PSU3B/4R	7200891	Plaxton	C53F	1972
RWW 977	94	Bristol LS5G	117036	E.C.W.	B45F	1956
RWW 985	95	Bristol LS5G	117053	E.C.W.	B45F	1956

NOTE — 8608EV, a Duple Yeoman C41F bodied Ford 570E Demonstrator was hired for a few weeks in Autumn 1961.

EXPLANATION OF SEATING LAYOUTS
B — Single-Deck Saloon
C — Coach
Ch — Charabanc
DP — Dual-Purpose Single-Deck (i.e. coach seating in bus shell)
F — Full-front where not normally fitted
H — Highbridge double-deck
L — Lowbridge double-deck (i.e. sunken side gangway upstairs)
O — Open-top double-deck
U — War-time Utility Bus
Seating capacities are given with the upper saloon first on d/ds.
D — Dual Doorway
D — (after entrance position) Platform doors where not normally fitted
F — Front entrance
OS — Open staircase
R — Rear entrance
8 — 8ft wide body where not normally fitted
- — Information not known

Into Service	Withdrawn	Purchased from	Sold to	Notes
5/68	5/69	County, Batford	Berger, London N7.	
8/68	6/72	Ribble MS 1357	Pennine MS (not run)	Sold for scrap
4/69	1/72	Scrivenor Lon. E10	Gray, Foehadois	
1/69	12/70	Yelloway, Rochdale	Kirby (dealer) N. Anston	
1/70	7/72	City of Oxford MS 968	Pennine MS (not run)	Platform doors fitted by Laycock
4/70	8/72	West Yorks. RCC SUG 32	Pennine MS (not run)	To Martin (dealer) Weaverham
11/70	8/72	Bristol OC 2892	Pennine MS (not run)	To Martin (dealer) Weaverham
11/70	8/72	Bristol OC 2893	Pennine MS (not run)	To Martin (dealer) Weaverham
3/71	4/72	Shirley, Meriden	Clarke, Goose Green	New to Gardiner, Spennymoor
3/71	1/72	Shirley, Meriden	Bingley, Kinsley (United)	New to Gardiner, Spennymoor
9/71	8/72	Bristol OC 2885	Pennine MS (not run)	To Martin (dealer) Weaverham
1/72	8/72	New	Pennine MS	
1/72	8/72	New	Pennine MS	
1/72	8/72	New	Pennine MS	
4/72	8/72	New	Pennine MS	
12/71	8/72	West Yorks. RCC SMG52	Pennine MS (not run)	To Martin (dealer) Weaverham
11/71	8/72	West Yorks. RCC SMG60	Pennine MS (not run)	To Martin (dealer) Weaverham

NOTES ON FLEET OWNERSHIP

2/05 — 1912   Messrs Ezra Laycock and W. Stephenson, trading as Laycock and Stephenson, Cowling

1912 — 23/10/33   Messrs Ezra, John and Rennie Laycock, trading as Ezra Laycock and Sons, Cowling

12/33 — 1/52   Messrs John and Rennie Laycock, joined later by Messrs Roy and Donald Laycock, trading as Ezra Laycock and Sons, Barnoldswick

1/52 — 12/8/72   Ezra Laycock Ltd., registered address West Close Road, Barnoldswick